# SPRING VALLEY

# DRUGS

# ALCOHOL

## A MyReportLinks.com Book

## Carl R. Green

MyReportLinks.com Books

an imprint of

 **Enslow Publishers, Inc.**

Box 398, 40 Industrial Road
Berkeley Heights, NJ 07922
USA

*Dedication*
*This book is lovingly dedicated to my parents,*
*who taught me all I'll ever need to know*
*about the use and misuse of alcohol*

MyReportLinks.com Books, an imprint of Enslow Publishers, Inc. MyReportLinks®
is a registered trademark of Enslow Publishers, Inc.

**Library of Congress Cataloging-in-Publication Data**

Green, Carl R.
  Alcohol  / Carl R. Green.
    p. cm. — (Drugs)
  Includes bibliographical references and index.
  ISBN 0-7660-5282-6
  1.  Drinking of alcoholic beverages—Juvenile literature. 2.  Alcohol—Juvenile literature. 3.
Alcoholism—Juvenile literature. I. Title.
  QP801.A3G74 2005
  613.81—dc22
                                    2004013797

Printed in the United States of America

10 9 8 7 6 5 4 3 2 1

**To Our Readers:**
Through the purchase of this book, you and your library gain access to the Report Links that specifically back
up this book.
The Publisher will provide access to the Report Links that back up this book and will keep these Report Links
up to date on **www.myreportlinks.com** for five years from the book's first publication date.
We have done our best to make sure all Internet addresses in this book were active and appropriate when we went
to press. However, the author and the Publisher have no control over, and assume no liability for, the material
available on those Internet sites or on other Web sites they may link to.
The usage of the MyReportLinks.com Books Web site is subject to the terms and conditions stated on the Usage
Policy Statement on **www.myreportlinks.com**.
A password may be required to access the Report Links that back up this book. The password is found on the
bottom of page 4 of this book.
Any comments or suggestions can be sent by e-mail to comments@myreportlinks.com or to the address on the
back cover.

**Photo Credits:** AlcoholScreening.org, p. 39; © 1996–2004, Eric H. Chudler, pp. 24, 26; © 2003 The Center
on Alcohol Marketing and Youth, p. 32; © 2004 Alcoholics Anonymous World Services, Inc., p. 37; © Mothers
Against Drunk Driving, p. 13; Digital Stock Government and Social Issues, pp. 3 (glass and keys), 35, 42;
Hemera Image Express, pp. 9, 14, 20; MyReportLinks.com Books, p. 4; National Cancer Institute/J. Troha,
p. 30; Photos.com, pp. 3 (sipping wine, teen drinking), 15, 22, 41; Stockbyte, p. 1; Stockbyte Sensitive Issues,
pp. 11, 19, 28, 34; Westerville Public Library, p. 17.

**Cover Photo:** Photos.com (whiskey glass); Stockbyte (distraught woman drinker).

**Disclaimer:** While the stories of abuse in this book are real, many of the names have been changed.

# MyReportLinks.com Books
## Great Books, Great Links, Great for Research!

The Internet sites listed on the next four pages can save you hours of research time. These Internet sites—we call them "Report Links"—are constantly changing, but we keep them up to date on our Web site.

Give it a try! Type http://www.myreportlinks.com into your browser, click on the series title, then the book title, and scroll down to the Report Links listed for this book.

The Report Links will bring you to great source documents, photographs, and illustrations. MyReportLinks.com Books save you time, feature Report Links that are kept up to date, and make report writing easier than ever!

Please see "To Our Readers" on the copyright page for important information about this book, the MyReportLinks.com Web site, and the Report Links that back up this book.

Please enter **DRA1123** if asked for a password.

The Internet sites described below can be accessed at
http://www.myreportlinks.com

### ▶Alcohol
*EDITOR'S CHOICE

Learn about alcohol and its effects on the nervous system, driving ability, and more. Calculate how many drinks you can have before you are over the legal limit to drive.

### ▶TeensHealth: Alcohol
*EDITOR'S CHOICE

The average American has his or her first alcoholic beverage around the age of fourteen. On this Web site, you will find information on how alcohol affects your body, reasons you should not drink, and where to get help if you or someone you know has a drinking problem.

### ▶Students Against Destructive Decisions (SADD)
*EDITOR'S CHOICE

Members of SADD are working to help their peers make good decisions in life, including decisions about alcohol. Learn about SADD, and read statistics on underage drinking.

### ▶NCADD Facts and Information
*EDITOR'S CHOICE

From the National Council on Alcoholism and Drug Dependence, this Web site provides interviews with drug experts, fact sheets on alcohol's effects, and a monthly question-and-answer column.

### ▶State-by-State Alcohol-Related Laws
*EDITOR'S CHOICE

On the Mothers Against Drunk Driving (MADD) Web site you can view a listing of alcohol-related laws that are in effect in each of the fifty states.

### ▶Tips for Teens: The Truth About Alcohol
*EDITOR'S CHOICE

This Web site clears up some myths about alcohol and provides a clear picture of the drug's effects, signs of abuse, and risks to your health.

## The Internet sites described below can be accessed at http://www.myreportlinks.com

### ▶Alcohol & Drug Information: For Kids Only

Learn about the warning signs of alcohol abuse and how to help people with alcohol problems at this Web site for kids.

### ▶Alcohol and Public Health

From the Centers for Disease Control and Prevention, this Web site provides statistics on alcohol abuse, drunk driving, and other alcohol-related problems. Read their FAQs on alcohol's effects.

### ▶Alcohol Concern

Great Britain has alcohol problems, too. This site investigates the social issues and criminal activities that grow out of alcohol abuse. Read about the demographics of this problem, and check out useful sources dealing with treatment and prevention.

### ▶Alcohol Screening.org

From Boston College, this site offers a screening tool for drinking problems. It also has fact sheets on alcohol abuse and resources for finding help.

### ▶Alcoholics Anonymous

Alcoholics Anonymous is one of the best-known help groups in the country. At its Web site you can read stories of alcohol abuse and recovery. Take a quiz to see if someone you know has an alcohol problem.

### ▶Anti-Saloon League: 1893–1933

The Westerville Public Library describes the history of the Anti-Saloon League and the temperance movement. View posters, pledge cards, and more at this Web site.

### ▶Ardent Spirits

View the history of the American temperance movement through pictures, engravings, and cartoons accompanied by detailed captions.

### ▶Benjamin Rush

Dickinson College outlines the life of early temperance advocate Benjamin Rush. Links to the full text of some of Rush's writings are provided.

Any comments? Contact us: **comments@myreportlinks.com**

## Report Links

### The Internet sites described below can be accessed at http://www.myreportlinks.com

▶**Center on Alcohol Marketing and Youth**

This Web site examines the advertising of alcohol, and analyzes some of the ads themselves. View research reports showing children's exposure to alcohol advertising.

▶**The Century Council**

The Century Council was formed in 1991 to reduce drunk driving and prevent illegal underage drinking. Learn more about this organization and its many projects.

▶**Community Health Promotion's Alcohol Awareness Site**

West Virginia University examines the history of alcohol and its affects on your body and society. Find out about fetal alcohol syndrome, alcoholism, treatment options, and more.

▶**The Cool Spot**

This Web site from the National Institute on Alcohol Abuse and Alcoholism posts recent studies pertaining to teenage drinking, as well as facts about alcohol. Learn how to resist peer pressure.

▶**Do It Now Foundation Publications: Alcohol & Alcoholism**

Read about alcohol's affects on the body, young people, and families. Learn about the warning signs of alcoholism and how to find help.

▶**Drink Smart**

Drink Smart features stories written by teenagers about the affects of alcohol on themselves and their families. Learn about the mistakes they made while drinking and how some people stopped.

▶**Drinking: It Can Spin Your World Around: Facts for Teens**

This Web site from the American Academy of Family Physicians contains facts that teens should know about alcohol. Information on the effects of alcohol on the body, as well as how to know if you have a problem with alcohol, are included.

▶**"Fetal Alcohol Syndrome" Quest**

This Centers for Disease Control and Prevention Web site describes fetal alcohol syndrome (FAS). You can read stories of people who suffer from FAS.

## Report Links

**The Internet sites described below can be accessed at http://www.myreportlinks.com**

### ▶Impaired Driving

From the National Center for Injury Prevention and Control comes a fact sheet on impaired driving. This sheet provides recent statistics on the injuries, deaths, and economic costs caused by drunk driving.

### ▶Kids and Alcohol

An interesting article written by doctors explains how alcohol affects your body and why drinking at a young age makes it more likely that you will grow up an alcoholic.

### ▶MADD: Stats and Resources

From Mothers Against Drunk Driving, this site provides statistics and research on drunk driving, underage drinking, and the cost of alcohol abuse. This site also spotlights prevention resources.

### ▶MADD: Under 21

This information about underage drinking is aimed at students from elementary school to college. Learn how underage drinking affects the drinker as well as those surrounding him or her. Find out how to protect yourself from those who drink irresponsibly and much more.

### ▶National Association for Children of Alcoholics: Just 4 Kids

Read about who is responsible for a parent's drinking and what a child can do about it. This site also contains a list of online and print resources.

### ▶National Hardcore Drunk Driver Project

See what can be done about the one percent of drivers involved in 50 percent of the fatal weekend crashes. This Web site also includes state profiles related to the identification and punishment of hardcore drunk drivers.

### ▶National Organization on Fetal Alcohol Syndrome

Produced by alcohol experts, this site gives information on fetal alcohol syndrome. Find statistics and useful lists of prevention efforts regarding FAS here.

### ▶State Drunk Driving Laws

This site provides state-by-state comparisons of drunk driving laws, including blood alcohol levels (BAC) and enhanced penalties for fatalities.

Any comments? Contact us: **comments@myreportlinks.com**

# ALCOHOL FACTS

✗ The scientific name for alcohol is ethanol. Its chemical formula is $CH_3CH_2OH$.

✗ Alcohol has a boiling point of 172°F (78°C) and a freezing point of −173°F (−114°C.)

✗ Many popular beverages contain alcohol. Among them are fermented drinks (beer, wine, hard cider, sake, ale, and malt liquor) and distilled drinks (whiskey, rum, brandy, vodka, and gin).

✗ Industrial and household products often contain alcohol, too. It is used as a solvent for lacquers, varnishes, and stains. It also is found in detergents, flavorings, and fragrances, and is added to gasoline to improve the octane rating.

✗ Drivers can be arrested for driving while intoxicated (DWI) if their blood alcohol concentration (BAC) exceeds the limit set by the state. Some of these limits are:

.01–.04 percent: may be DWI; illegal if under age twenty-one.

.05–.07 percent: likely DWI; illegal if under age twenty-one.

.08 percent and up: definitely DWI.

✗ 31 percent of Americans say that drinking has caused trouble in their families.

✗ 44.9 percent of teenagers have used alcohol in the past month.

✗ 28.3 percent of teenagers engaged in binge drinking in the past month.

✗ 12.1 percent of teenagers admit to drinking and driving.

✗ The number of sixteen- to twenty-year-olds killed in drunk-driving crashes in 2002 was 1,881.

✗ The states with the highest percentage of underage drinkers are North Dakota, Massachusetts, and New Hampshire.

✗ The states with the lowest percentage of underage drinkers include Utah, Virginia, and Mississippi.

✗ Alcohol is a drug. It harms more people than all other drugs combined.

✗ Many think alcohol will give them a quick pick-me-up. The fact is, alcohol is a depressant. The brief lift it offers soon gives way to muddled thinking and lethargy.

✗ Only time can sober you up—an hour per drink for most people.

# "WHY NOT ME?"

**Have** you had a talk like this with yourself? The chances are good that you will, sooner or later. Here is how it might sound:

**Voice in your head:** *"Hey, your friends just offered you a can of beer! Why did you turn it down?"*

**You:** *"It's no big deal. This is a great party. I don't need alcohol to enjoy myself."*

**Voice:** *"What, you call this a good time? You're just sitting here, completely clueless. A little beer will loosen you up. You might even break down and ask someone to dance."*

**You:** *"You're right, it's not much fun here on the sidelines. But I promised Mom and Dad that I wouldn't drink until I'm twenty-one."*

**Voice:** *"What Mom and Dad don't know won't hurt them! Besides, it's no big deal. Just reach into that cooler, grab a can, and pop the top. You'll soon feel like a million bucks."*

**You:** *"Gee, I don't know. Well . . . maybe just this once. Everyone else is having a blast! Why not me?"*

That is the heart of the matter, is it not? Why not me? Before you reach into that cooler, though, you might want to think again. There are a number of good reasons to say "No, thanks," when someone offers you a drink.

## ▶ Alcohol Is a Drug

The law is quite clear: Your local mini-mart would be shut down in an instant if it tried to sell drugs like heroin and cocaine. No one, however, objects when that same mini-mart sells beer, whiskey, wine, and other alcoholic drinks to adult shoppers. That is a bit weird, when you stop and think about it, because like cocaine, alcohol is a drug, and a very addictive drug at that. Like its hard-drug cousins, alcohol does more than alter mood and behavior . . . an overdose can kill.

▲ Some people talk themselves into having a drink when they know that they probably should not. Will this man be able to keep his job if he shows up at work with alcohol on his breath? Probably not.

The issue seems quite clear to everyone who works to help alcohol's victims: If alcoholic beverages were handled like the drugs they are, you would need a prescription to buy them. In bold print, each label would warn users not to use alcohol while driving or operating machinery. Along with describing a number of possible side effects, the warning would emphasize alcohol's addictive properties.

Once this powerful drug hits your bloodstream, it heads straight to your brain. Almost at once, you start to feel a bit "tipsy." This relaxed and powerful feeling comes at the expense of balance, coordination, and judgment. Over time, the body will need more and more alcohol to regain that "high."

Is there a price to pay for these brief flights from reality? Let's see what happened to Ashley, Terry, Crista, and Joaquin.

## The High Price of Getting High

*Ashley.** The party was in full swing, and Ashley was ready to have some fun. To overcome her shyness, the teenager gulped down several glasses of wine. "The real Ashley comes out after I have a few drinks," she told her friends. This "real" Ashley was the life of the party right up to the time she collapsed on the floor. Someone called the paramedics, who took her to the hospital. On the way, she threw up all over herself. A pale and shaken Ashley was left to cope with a dreadful hangover and the knowledge that she could have died if her friends had not called 911 so quickly.[1]

*Terry.* To celebrate their star goalie's birthday, Terry's soccer teammates threw a party on the eve of their big game. The coolers were stocked with plenty of beer, and Terry lost track of how many bottles he chugalugged. He awoke the next day with a dry mouth and a headache, but he sneaked a beer out of the fridge and that seemed to help. As game time drew near, Terry felt a bit sluggish, but no one seemed to notice. The game was a different matter. Shots that Terry normally stopped with ease flew past his

*Disclaimer: While the stories of abuse in this book are real, many of the names have been changed.

**Motor Vehicle Traffic Fatalities During Prom / Graduation Weekends - 2000**

Statistics
- General Statistics
- By State
- By Holiday
- Fatalities
- Children
- Youth Statistics
- The Brain
- Minimum Drinking Age Laws
- Arrests
- BAC
- Economic Costs
- Diverse Populations
- By Age
- By Gender
- Pedestrians
- Occupant Protection
- Alcohol Advertising
- Repeat Offenders
- References

Laws
Drunk Driving Research
Underage Drinking Research

| Prom / Graduation Dates | Total Traffic Fatalities | Total Fatalities Alcohol-Related | Percent Alcohol-Related |
|---|---|---|---|
| 4/14/00 - 4/16/00 (6:00 pm Friday to 5:59 pm Sunday) | 215 | 137 | 63.9% |
| 4/21/00 - 4/23/00 (6:00 pm Friday to 5:59 pm Sunday) | 207 | 117 | 56.7% |
| 4/28/00 - 4/30/00 (6:00 pm Friday to 5:59 pm Sunday) | 225 | 131 | 58.3% |
| 5/5/00 - 5/7/00 (6:00 pm Friday to 5:59 pm Sunday) | 246 | 136 | 55.2% |
| 5/12/00 - 5/14/00 (6:00 pm Friday to 5:59 pm Sunday) | 237 | 140 | 58.9% |
| 5/19/00 - 5/21/00 (6:00 pm Friday to 5:59 pm Sunday) | 234 | 142 | 60.6% |
| 6/2/00 - 6/4/00 (6:00 pm Friday to 5:59 pm Sunday) | 240 | 138 | 57.4% |
| 6/9/00 - 6/11/00 (6:00 pm Friday to 5:59 pm Sunday) | 268 | 163 | 60.9% |
| 6/16/00 - 6/18/00 (6:00 pm Friday to 5:59 pm Sunday) | 210 | 122 | 58% |

*There were more alcohol-related traffic deaths on the weekend of June 9 through June 11, 2000, than any other prom or graduation weekend that year. Alcohol played a part in almost 61 percent of the total traffic fatalities during that three-day span.*

outstretched fingers. When the coach asked him what was wrong, he could only shake his head. No one had warned him that the aftereffects of getting drunk include impaired coordination, slow reaction times—and a seat on the bench for the second half.[2]

*Crista:* Crista started drinking to ease the pain of watching her father drown himself in alcohol. The habit came easily, for she had been sampling his drinks since she was five. By her junior year, she was drinking every weekend. Crista was driving by this time, and sometimes drove when she was drunk. Despite some close calls, she somehow managed to avoid having an accident. Later, after spending time in a halfway house to try to kick her addiction, Crista described her painful feelings of guilt. "First I'd wake up in the morning, hung over and feeling sick. Then I'd think, 'It was only by the grace of God that I got home without killing myself or anyone else,'" she confessed to her counselor.[3]

*Joaquin:* High school senior Joaquin did not learn Crista's lesson until it was too late. With school about to start, Joaquin and his friends drove to his dad's mountain cabin for a party weekend. Saturday slipped by, full of sun, poker, and plenty of beer. That night, everyone ate hotdogs, danced, and drank more beer. About one o'clock in the morning, Joaquin climbed into his car and drove to the nearby town to buy gas. On the trip back, his brain fogged by alcohol, he lost control and plowed into a pickup full of teenagers. One girl died in the crash, and two boys were badly injured. Charged with drunk driving and manslaughter, Joaquin was put on trial as an adult and convicted. A no-nonsense judge sentenced him to twenty years in prison.

Now you know what Ashley, Ben, Crista, and Joaquin should have said when they were offered a drink. "Thanks, but I'll stick to the soft stuff," is a pretty good place to start.

◀ Getting behind the wheel of a car after a few shots of alcohol can turn into a deadly experience. It is best to hand your keys over to a designated driver if you have been drinking.

**Chapter 2** ▶

# A LONG AND CHECKERED HISTORY

**Humanity's** use (and misuse) of intoxicants predates history. Of all the thousands of organized societies that have lived on this planet, only the Inuit people did not smoke, drink, or snort mind-altering substances. The reason, anthropologists note, was environmental, not cultural. Crops simply did not grow in the Inuit's Arctic habitat.[1]

As for alcohol, humans have been drinking fermented beverages for thousands of years. In 2001, a search team in Syria dug up a cache of clay tablets. A translation of the ancient writing told the diggers that they had unearthed a thirty-eight hundred-year-old recipe for making beer. A second set of tablets told them how much beer the long-vanished brewers had produced.[2]

*People have been drinking wine since* ▶ *ancient times. Back then, wine was often safer than water because alcoholic drinks are less likely to play host to disease-causing bacteria.*

Early cultures used myths to explain the origins of beer and wine. A story from Persia (modern Iran) tells of a king who stored his grape harvest in large clay jars. As time passed, the juice fermented into a crude wine. Fearing that it was poisonous, no one drank the potent liquid. Months later, a slave wracked by headaches tried to kill herself by drinking the "poison." Instead of dying, she found that the drink eased her pain. Hearing the story, the king tasted the wine and declared that it was good. "Plant more grapes. We need more of this royal medicine!" he told his people.[3]

Wine and civilization seemed to march in lockstep. The Bible tells us that Noah planted a vineyard soon after he landed on Mount Ararat. Wine came to Greece around 2,000 B.C. and quickly became a favorite drink. In their own time, the Romans copied the custom. During the Gallic wars, Julius Caesar issued a daily ration of wine to his soldiers. Drinking wine, he said, would prevent the soldiers from getting dysentery (an infectious disease that causes severe diarrhea). Back home, Roman citizens guarded their health by drinking wine with their meals. In those days, it was a safer drink than water from a polluted stream or well.[4]

## ▶ America's Love-Hate Affair With Alcohol

The colonists who settled the New World brought their love of strong drink with them. The Puritans were no exception. The hardy men and women who sailed on the *Mayflower* carried more beer than water in the ship's hold. Later, at the first Thanksgiving, they washed down the feast with cups of beer, brandy, gin, and wine.[5] Village elders sentenced drunks to the stocks, but not because of their drinking. A far worse sin, in Puritan eyes, was failing to get one's work done.[6]

As the country grew, alcohol tightened its grip. Taverns sprang up in every town and village. In off hours, the taverns served as courtrooms and churches. "Alcohol," one writer noted, "sustained the sailor and plowman, the trader and trapper. By it were lighted the fires of revelry and of devotion. Few doubted that it was a great boon to mankind." In 1678, mourners at a Boston funeral paid tribute to that "great boon" by downing 50 gallons (189 liters) of wine.[7] Revolutionary War soldiers drew a daily ration of 4 ounces (11.8 centiliters) of rum or whiskey.

With freedom came a lively new debate. Church leaders took to their pulpits to preach the evils of "demon rum." Even so, their pleas for an end to public drunkenness mostly fell on deaf ears. Only American Indians, victims of the myth that "firewater" turned them into wild, murderous brutes, were forbidden to drink. In 1795, Dr. Benjamin Rush added fuel to the temperance (antialcohol) movement. Rush was far ahead of his time when he labeled alcoholism "a disease." The only cure, he warned, was to stop drinking.[8]

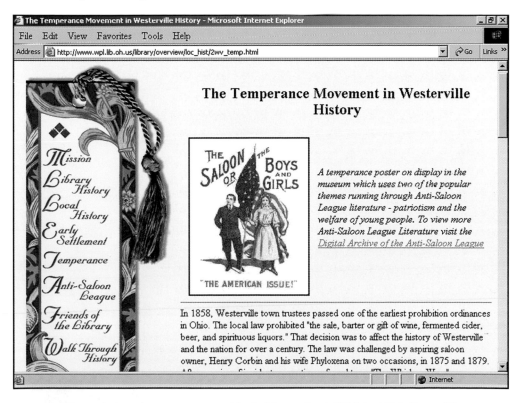

▲ The early temperance movement lasted from about 1800 to 1890. One of the most active groups during this time was the Anti-Saloon League. It used posters such as this one to get out its message regarding the evils of alcohol.

The hard-drinking nation paid little attention to the good doctor's advice. By 1830, the average American was drinking 5 gallons (18.9 liters) of alcohol a year.[9] The solution, alcohol's foes said, was to prohibit the selling of alcoholic drinks. Antialcohol groups such as the Anti-Saloon League pressured the states to pass new laws. By 1917, when the United States entered World War I, twenty-six states had gone "dry." The next step was national prohibition, which arrived with the Eighteenth Amendment to the Constitution in 1920. Almost at once, it became clear that the public held the new law in contempt. Gangsters quickly took up the task of selling bootleg whiskey and gin. Efforts to enforce the law floundered in the face of public scorn.

In 1932, the nation heaved a sigh of relief as Prohibition passed into history. Repeal handed control back to the states. The states, in turn, passed their own liquor-control laws. Each state went its own way, but all agreed on one key point. Alcohol, the states ruled, must be kept out of the hands of children and teenagers.

## ▶ A Focus on Reform

Is underage drinking really a serious issue? Take a look at some scary numbers before you answer that question.

- Ten million teenagers drink monthly and 8 million drink weekly. Of that number, over 500,000 teens go on weekly binges of five or more drinks in a row.

- High school students consume 102 million gallons (386 million liters) of beer per year.

- Studies show that teen drinkers cut classes, get into fights, and commit vandalism.

- In 2002, 1,881 teenagers died in teen drunk-driving crashes. Alcohol also plays a role in many teen suicides and shootings.

- Underage drinking costs the nation $53 billion a year.[10]

▲ *Underage drinking has become a problem throughout the United States. In 2002, almost nineteen-hundred teens died in accidents involving drunk drivers. Alcohol abuse affects coordination and alertness.*

The National Research Council issued two strong proposals in 2003. The first step, the council said, is for both adults and the alcohol industry to clean up their acts. Parents, for instance, must keep a closer watch on their sons and daughters. Young people, studies show, obtain most of their alcohol from adults. For its

▲ When young people view television commercials for alcoholic beverages, they usually see successful people having the time of their lives. The reality is that alcoholism and alcohol abuse can lead to crippling depression and despair.

part, the industry must make sure that its advertising does not target teenagers. In one survey, more than half of the teens said that beer commercials encouraged them to drink.[11]

The council's second proposal zeroed in on alcohol taxes. Tobacco taxes have soared in recent years, but alcohol taxes are unchanged. Whiskey is taxed at $2.14 a bottle. The beer tax is much lower at only thirty-three cents a six-pack, and the wine tax raises only twenty-one cents a bottle. Increasing these taxes will help in two ways, the council believes. First, anything that makes booze (alcohol) more expensive will tend to discourage teen drinking. Second, higher taxes can be used to fund tough anti-drinking campaigns.[12]

The industry that makes and sells alcoholic beverages agrees only in part. Yes, underage drinking must be controlled, industry leaders say. We do our part, they claim, by not aiming our advertising at teenagers. When it comes to higher taxes, they claim that cost has little to do with keeping teens away from alcohol. Determined young people, the companies argue, will always find ways to buy, beg, or steal a can or bottle.

Only when it comes to teaching young people about alcohol's use and misuse do the two sides see eye to eye. In that light, let us take a close look at alcohol and its effects.

# MEET THE WORLD'S "DIRTIEST DRUG"

**Ask** yourself, how can something that makes you feel so good be so unhealthy? A gifted writer named Jack London never did figure it out. At times he cursed his love of strong drink. At other times, he saw drinking as a "gorgeous episode in the monotony of life and labor." He was still wrestling with his addiction when he died of kidney failure at age forty.[1]

What is this substance that antialcohol crusader Ernest Noble calls "the dirtiest drug of all"?[2] Chemists know it as $CH_3CH_2OH$, or ethanol. In less polite circles, alcohol is sometimes called "yeast poop." The phrase is pretty much on target. When tiny yeast organisms meet the plant sugars found in fruits, grains, and berries, they go right to work. In a process known as fermentation, the yeast "eats" the sugars and excretes them as carbon dioxide and alcohol. In wine, the process dies out when the alcohol content rises to about 14 percent. To make a stronger drink, distillers heat

◀ *Whiskey and other hard liquors have a lot of alcohol in a small quantity. A jigger of whiskey—1.5 ounces (4.7 centiliters)—contains as much alcohol as a 12-ounce (1.9 centiliter) can of beer.*

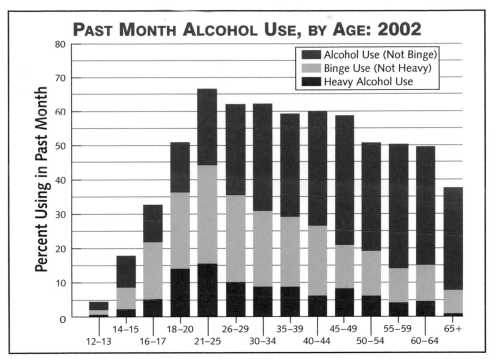

PAST MONTH ALCOHOL USE, BY AGE: 2002

Legend:
- Alcohol Use (Not Binge)
- Binge Use (Not Heavy)
- Heavy Alcohol Use

Y-axis: Percent Using in Past Month

X-axis: 12–13, 14–15, 16–17, 18–20, 21–25, 26–29, 30–34, 35–39, 40–44, 45–49, 50–54, 55–59, 60–64, 65+

Source: 2002 National Survey on Drug Use and Health, Substance Abuse and Mental Health Services Administration

the sugary liquid. As the alcohol boils away, the vapor is captured and condensed. Next, to tempt human taste buds, the distillers add color and flavor. Each recipe calls for a different mix of sugars, spices, and other types of alcohol.[3]

Some alcoholic drinks are stronger than others. Whiskey and gin are about 40 percent alcohol. Wine averages 12 percent, and beer checks in at 5 percent. Anyone who takes a drink should keep these equivalents in mind:

**Whiskey:** 01.5 oz (04.7 centiliters) = .60 oz (1.9 centiliters) alcohol

**Wine:** 05.0 oz (15.6 centiliters) = .60 oz (1.9 centiliters) alcohol

**Beer:** 12.0 oz (37.5 centiliters) = .60 oz (1.9 centiliters) alcohol[4]

Once people take a drink, alcohol gets right to work. If they stop with that one drink, its effects on the brain and body last

Neuroscience for Kids - Alcohol - Microsoft Internet Explorer

File   Edit   View   Favorites   Tools   Help

Address   http://faculty.washington.edu/chudler/alco.html

## ALCOHOL IMPAIRMENT CHART

N E V E R   D R I N K   A N D   D R I V E

### APPROXIMATE BLOOD ALCOHOL PERCENTAGE

| Drinks | Body Weight in Pounds | | | | | | | | | |
|---|---|---|---|---|---|---|---|---|---|---|
| | 90 | 100 | 120 | 140 | 160 | 180 | 200 | 220 | 240 | |
| 0 | .00 | .00 | .00 | .00 | .00 | .00 | .00 | .00 | .00 | ONLY SAFE DRIVING LIMIT |
| 1 | .05 | .05 | .04 | .03 | .03 | .03 | .02 | .02 | .02 | IMPAIRMENT BEGINS |
| 2 | .10 | .09 | .08 | .07 | .06 | .05 | .05 | .04 | .04 | DRIVING SKILLS |
| 3 | .15 | .14 | .11 | .10 | .09 | .08 | .07 | .06 | .06 | SIGNIFICANTLY AFFECTED |
| 4 | .20 | .18 | .15 | .13 | .11 | .10 | .09 | .08 | .08 | — POSSIBLE CRIMINAL PENALTIES |
| 5 | .25 | .23 | .19 | .16 | .14 | .13 | .11 | .10 | .09 | |
| 6 | .30 | .27 | .23 | .19 | .17 | .15 | .14 | .12 | .11 | |
| 7 | .35 | .32 | .27 | .23 | .20 | .18 | .16 | .14 | .13 | LEGALLY INTOXICATED |
| 8 | .40 | .36 | .30 | .26 | .23 | .20 | .18 | .17 | .15 | — CRIMINAL PENALTIES |
| 9 | .45 | .41 | .34 | .29 | .26 | .23 | .20 | .19 | .17 | |
| 10 | .51 | .45 | .38 | .32 | .28 | .25 | .23 | .21 | .19 | |

Your body can get rid of one drink per hour.
One 1½ oz. of 80 proof liquor, 12 oz. of beer or 5 oz. of table wine = 1 drink.

Pennsylvania Liquor Control Board
In The Public Interest

Done                                          Internet

▲ Almost all females are affected by just one alcoholic beverage. For some, a second drink makes them legally intoxicated.

about an hour. With each new drink, the effect grows stronger and lasts longer. Chemistry, however, is only a small part of the story. What really counts is the effect this toxic drug has on thoughts, feelings, and actions.

## ▶ Jack Takes a Drink

As a teenager, Jack often downed seven or eight drinks in a row. One night he fell and gashed his face, but even then he refused to admit that he had a problem. "For nearly two years, my life revolved around the bottle," he says. "What really gets me now is that I actually thought I was having fun."[5]

Jack finally got the message the morning he woke up lying in a pool of his own vomit. The first step was to stop drinking. Then he set out to learn what alcohol had been doing to his body. The more he read, the more he regretted drinking in the first place.

Alcohol begins to affect you the moment you take the first sip. Women and girls feel the effect faster because their body chemistry pushes up their blood alcohol content (BAC) more quickly. Even so, the results are much the same for both sexes. When you swallow, about 10 percent of the alcohol is absorbed into the bloodstream through the lining of the mouth and throat. Another 20 percent enters the blood through the stomach. The final 70 percent is absorbed through the walls of the small intestine. Age, weight, gender, and amount of body fat all play a role in the body's response. As more alcohol reaches the bloodstream, your BAC ratchets upward. A BAC of .10 means that the body has one part alcohol per every one thousand parts blood.[6] In California, police arrest adults for drunk driving who show a BAC of .08 or more. Teenage drivers lose their licenses if tests show a BAC of .01 or more.

## Feeling the Effects

Alcohol is classed as a depressant, but it hits each of us in slightly different ways. In general, when alcohol first reaches the brain, people feel relaxed and happy. At a party, noise levels rise and shy loners perk up. People who continue to drink tend to lose concentration and become sleepy. As their BAC levels rise, speech becomes slurred and motor skills suffer. At BACs of .40 and above, the once happy drunk is likely to pass out. To drinkers who plead for a quick way to sober up, doctors can only shake their heads. No amount of coffee, exercise, food, or magic herbs will do the job. Only time and the metabolic processes carried on by the liver can bring BAC levels back to zero.[7]

Waking up the next day, drinkers often find that alcohol has left its calling card. Nondrinkers joke about the painful symptoms of a classic hangover. The hangover's victims seldom see the humor. The loss of body fluids and high alkaline levels caused by

## ALCOHOL IMPAIRMENT CHART

**NEVER DRINK AND DRIVE**

### APPROXIMATE BLOOD ALCOHOL PERCENTAGE

| Drinks | Body Weight in Pounds | | | | | | | | |
|---|---|---|---|---|---|---|---|---|---|
| | 100 | 120 | 140 | 160 | 180 | 200 | 220 | 240 | |
| 0 | .00 | .00 | .00 | .00 | .00 | .00 | .00 | .00 | ONLY SAFE DRIVING LIMIT |
| 1 | .04 | .03 | .03 | .02 | .02 | .02 | .02 | .02 | IMPAIRMENT BEGINS |
| 2 | .08 | .06 | .05 | .05 | .04 | .04 | .03 | .03 | |
| 3 | .11 | .09 | .08 | .07 | .06 | .06 | .05 | .05 | DRIVING SKILLS SIGNIFICANTLY AFFECTED |
| 4 | .15 | .12 | .11 | .09 | .08 | .08 | .07 | .06 | |
| 5 | .19 | .16 | .13 | .12 | .11 | .09 | .09 | .08 | POSSIBLE CRIMINAL PENALTIES |
| 6 | .23 | .19 | .16 | .14 | .13 | .11 | .10 | .09 | |
| 7 | .26 | .22 | .19 | .16 | .15 | .13 | .12 | .11 | LEGALLY INTOXICATED |
| 8 | .30 | .25 | .21 | .19 | .17 | .15 | .14 | .13 | |
| 9 | .34 | .28 | .24 | .21 | .19 | .17 | .15 | .14 | CRIMINAL PENALTIES |
| 10 | .38 | .31 | .27 | .23 | .21 | .19 | .17 | .16 | |

Your body can get rid of one drink per hour.
One 1½ oz. of 80 proof liquor, 12 oz. of beer or 5 oz. of table wine = 1 drink.

▲ Most teenagers are surprised when they learn that almost all males are affected by just one alcoholic drink.

heavy drinking lead to any number of painful symptoms. The worst symptoms include a throbbing headache, a raging thirst, and stomach-churning nausea. Sunlight blinds the eyes. Even minor noises threaten to split one's skull. When hangover victims try to recall the night before, they often come up with a blank.[8]

## ▶ Stay Off the "Drinking Wheel"

Jack kicked his love affair with alcohol none too soon. Each drinking binge left him teetering on the edge of the addiction called alcoholism. No one knows for sure what fluke of body chemistry might have pushed Jack over the edge. Some scientists suspect that the answer to that question will be found in our genes. Their research suggests that heredity tilts 10 to 15 percent of us toward alcohol addiction.[9] Dr. Raymond Haring, a leader in the battle against alcohol abuse, describes the peril in terms of taking a trip on the "drinking wheel." A drinker's progress around the wheel, Haring writes, starts with the very first drink. From there, each use of alcohol to "relax" or "have fun" moves the drinker closer to a full-fledged addiction. For heavy drinkers, repeated binges speed up the process. Before they realize what has happened, alcohol has taken command of their lives.[10]

Talk to any recovering alcoholic, and they will utter a similar vow. "I am an alcoholic," Barry will tell you. "There may be people who can 'take it or leave it alone,' but I am not one of them. For my own sake and the sake of those I love, I can never take another drink. That is the price I pay for staying alive and healthy."

## ▷ Damage Done

Barry has it right. People who become addicted to alcohol endanger themselves and others. Some drunks make headlines by crashing their cars. Analysts also warn that drinkers are more likely to start fires. The lucky ones avoid the accidents but cannot escape alcohol's impact on their health and their family's well-being. Over time, alcohol damage to the brain can cause hallucinations (imaginary sights and sounds). High blood pressure can lead to a stroke or heart attack. A few heavy drinkers die of alcohol poisoning when their livers can no longer handle the toxins alcohol adds to their bodies. Alcoholics who survive these dangers have little cause to rejoice. Poor eating habits often leave their bodies starved of vitamins and minerals. In time, addiction to alcohol can severely weaken the immune system. Left with little protection from infection, alcoholics often die of cancer, AIDS, or some other fatal disease.

Deep in their alcoholic haze, heavy drinkers seldom worry about others. A drunk driver swerves and wipes out a family on its way to church. A teenage mom hits the bottle—and hits her

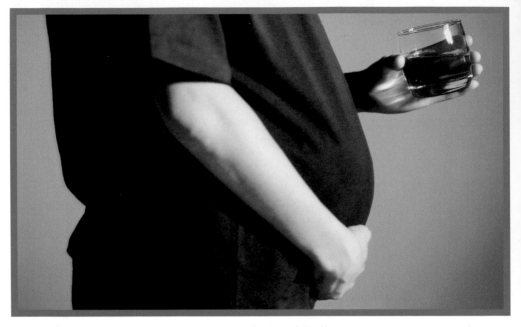

▲ Alcohol use can have an extremely harmful affect on a pregnant woman's fetus. Drinking can cause FAS, the third leading cause of birth defects.

toddler for crying too much. A salesman drinks too much at lunch and loses a big contract.

Those are tragic examples, but one newborn has an even sadder story to tell. Sam was born with a deformed face and shows signs of mental retardation. The cause: fetal alcohol syndrome (FAS). His mother promised to stop drinking while she was pregnant, but never did. Each shot of whiskey flooded Sam's system with crippling doses of alcohol. At birth, he joined some five thousand FAS babies born in the United States each year.[11] Doctors rank FAS as the third leading cause of birth defects. Those babies could have been born healthy, they add, if the mothers had given up alcohol for at least nine months.

Sadly, no one can "cure" alcoholism. If the research is correct, addiction starts with the first drink for those people who are genetically programmed to succumb. As recovering alcoholics know all too well, abstinence is the only cure.

**Chapter 4 ▶**

# ALCOHOL IN THE MARKETPLACE

**The** well-dressed men and women gather around the tasting table. Their host uncorks a bottle, sniffs the cork, and begins to pour. The tasters pick up their glasses and sniff the amber liquid. Then they take a small sip, swallow, and sigh with pleasure. The wine has passed the test. The tasters hold out their glasses for refills.

Deep in a nearby alley, two homeless men are holding their own wine tasting. The older man pulls a bottle from his coat and unscrews the cap. He takes a long, choking swallow. As he gasps for air, his buddy grabs the bottle and takes an even longer gulp. After a pause to exchange high fives, the two get down to work. A few minutes later, the first man tilts the bottle skyward and lets the last drops trickle down his throat.

There is nothing new about these two scenes. Humans took a liking to alcohol on the day our ancestors first sampled fermented grape juice. Today, instead of hiding their passion for strong drink, people celebrate it. Watch for the proof the next time you go to a wedding reception. When the best man calls for a toast, the waiters pour champagne, not grape juice. No matter what they say, it is not the taste that hooks people. The lure is the feelings of pleasure that alcohol triggers when it reaches the brain. Young people are no exception. Alcohol ranks ahead of tobacco and marijuana as the drug of choice among teens.[1]

## ▶ Money Talks

Think about the last beer commercial you watched. Perhaps it starred some cute bullfrogs or some tough cowhands. Did it make

▲ *Heavy use of alcohol can also speed up the aging process. Men and women who drink to excess often have sallow, wrinkled skin that makes them look far older than others their age.*

drinking beer look like a risky thing to do? Or did it make drinking look like a sexy, grown-up way to relax?

Clearly, the folks who sell alcohol slant their sales pitches. In 2002, for example, beer companies spent $58 million to run commercials during college sports broadcasts. As Bud Light's parent company explains, "We want to be where our customers are." Yet 40 percent of college students are under twenty-one and cannot legally purchase their products. The industry seems determined to ignore the fact that drinking has a darker side. The police link alcohol to the deaths of some fourteen hundred college students each year.[2]

Some public health experts believe that higher taxes would reduce teenage drinking and alcohol-related traffic deaths. When members of Congress propose any bill that affects alcohol sales, however, the industry springs into action. In 1996, for example, Joseph Kennedy sponsored a bill to put limits on how alcoholic beverages are advertised. "We spend $15 billion in a war on drugs," he said, "but then allow an industry to tell young people if they want to . . . win a bike race, they ought to go suck a brew." Thanks to the pressure placed on Congress by the liquor industry's lobbyists, his bill went nowhere. As a spokeswoman for Mothers Against Drunk Driving (MADD) explains, "Safety doesn't talk down here [in Congress]. Money talks."[3]

## ▶ Why Do So Many Kids Drink?

Every group has a different name for it. Some kids talk about getting "blitzed," "ripped," or "wasted." Others laugh about getting "smashed" or "high." Call it what you like—at times it seems as if everyone is doing it. The fact is, slightly less than half of the kids are fooling around with alcohol. In 2003, 44.9 percent of the students surveyed said they had taken one drink or more during the past month. The statistics on binge drinking were even more troubling. Nearly three in ten admitted to downing five or more drinks in a row at least once during the past month.[4]

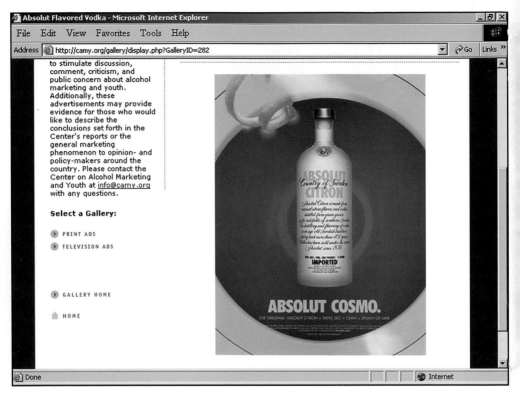

to stimulate discussion, comment, criticism, and public concern about alcohol marketing and youth. Additionally, these advertisements may provide evidence for those who would like to describe the conclusions set forth in the Center's reports or the general marketing phenomenon to opinion- and policy-makers around the country. Please contact the Center on Alcohol Marketing and Youth at info@camy.org with any questions.

**Select a Gallery:**

PRINT ADS

TELEVISION ADS

GALLERY HOME

HOME

▲ Over 12 percent of eighth graders are considered heavy drinkers. This number jumps to over 28 percent for high school seniors. Research has shown that more alcohol advertising, such as the ad shown here, reaches underage youth than adults.

Most teenagers know that underage drinking is illegal. They also know that it is bad for their health. Yet they keep on saying "yes" when someone hands them a drink. Why? There is no single answer to that question, just a shopping list of likely reasons. See if any of these ring a bell.

- *Allie drinks because her parents do.* "I admire my parents, and I want to grow up to be like them. Since they drink now and then, it must be an okay thing to do."

- *Connor drinks to relieve stress.* "Mom and dad take a drink or two at night to 'unwind.' Heck, I have lots of stress, too. So, why shouldn't I sneak a drink now and then?"

- *Kaitlyn drinks to be part of the "in" crowd.* "The kids I hang out with all drink. How can I say 'No' when someone breaks out a bottle? If I do, my friends won't like me any more."

- *Justin drinks to have fun.* "My 'party animal' doesn't come out until I've had a few drinks. If I stay cold sober, I just hide in the corner while my friends are having a good time."

- *Brianne drinks to forget.* "My parents fight a lot, and nothing I do seems to please them. When things get too crazy, I drink a glass or two of my dad's vodka to ease the hurt."

- *Kyle drinks because it makes him feel grown up.* "I'll be going off to college next year, right? I know I'll have to be able to hold my liquor if I want to fit in on campus."

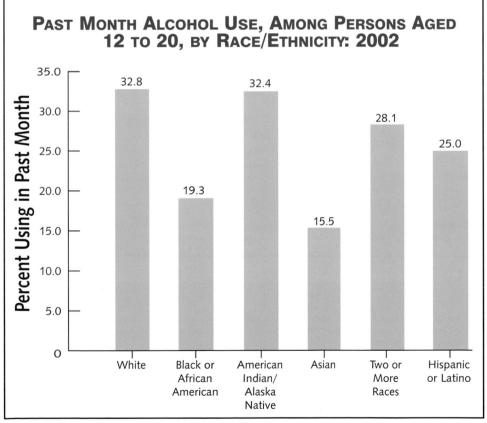

**PAST MONTH ALCOHOL USE, AMONG PERSONS AGED 12 TO 20, BY RACE/ETHNICITY: 2002**

*Source: 2002 National Survey on Drug Use and Health, Substance Abuse and Mental Health Services Administration*

How many kids would echo these six voices? No one can say for sure, but a group known as Alcohol Free Kids (AFK) thinks the facts speak for themselves. Alcohol, AFK says, is the drug of choice for young people. High school students consume millions of gallons of beer and wine coolers each year. More and more,

▲ Young people have begun to drink at earlier and earlier ages. Some are influenced by advertising, others are trying to imitate an older friend or relative who drinks regularly.

kids as young as eleven and twelve are joining the drinking crowd. The bottom line, AFK reminds us, is that alcohol will kill thousands of these young drinkers. Many of them will die before they reach the legal drinking age.[5]

## Fighting Back

Alcohol plays no favorites. Its dire effects can be found in every community, in every racial and ethnic group. Some teens abuse alcohol but stop short of becoming alcoholics. Others slip quickly into alcohol's addictive grasp. A third group must cope with the trauma of living with family members who abuse alcohol. Fortunately, most communities have resources for young people who need help.

Groups such as Alcohol Free Kids focus on the issue of drunk driving. AFK reminds us that more Americans have died in drunk-driving crashes than have died in the nation's wars. Underage drinking, the group warns, plays a major role in filling those graves. The answer? We must declare war on the causes of this "national

*Alateen is an organization that helps teens deal with issues related to alcohol abuse. Whether it is a family member with a drinking problem or a personal problem, groups such as Alateen can help you overcome them.*

emergency." The first step? Teach the nation's young people that one rule, at least, is absolute: *If you drink, do not drive!* [6]

Alateen is a branch of Al-Anon, the national organization that helps families and friends of alcoholics. The teenagers who join an Alateen support group meet once a week to discuss issues related to alcohol abuse. Many of the members need help in learning to cope with someone else's drinking. The children of alcoholics hear the message that they are not the cause of their parents' poor life choices. Teens who fear they might become alcoholics get the help they need to regain control. Most of all, Alateen members take comfort in knowing they are not alone, as do the members of Alcoholics Anonymous (AA). [7]

Almost every town and city supports at least one chapter of AA. This well-known self-help group, founded in 1935, pioneered the technique of bringing alcoholics together to help each other kick their addictions. At a typical meeting, a teenage girl looks her fellow AA'ers in the eye and says, "Hi, my name is Tanya and I'm an alcoholic." Then, choking back tears, she describes her long struggle with alcohol. As she ends her story, Tanya smiles as she tells her new friends, "I've been sober for three weeks now." Even if Tanya had been sober for three years, AA's Twelve Steps would caution her that she can never take another drink. The bottom line, AA members agree, can be stated in six words: "Once an alcoholic, always an alcoholic."

# LEARN FROM THE MISTAKES OF OTHERS

**In** grade school, Vic studied hard, made good grades, and played Little League baseball. Anxious to be seen as one of the cool guys, he took his first drink the night of his eighth-grade graduation. After that, Vic never looked back. In high school, he ran with a circle of older boys who smoked, drove fast cars, and drank too much. His grades slipped, and he was cut from the baseball team.

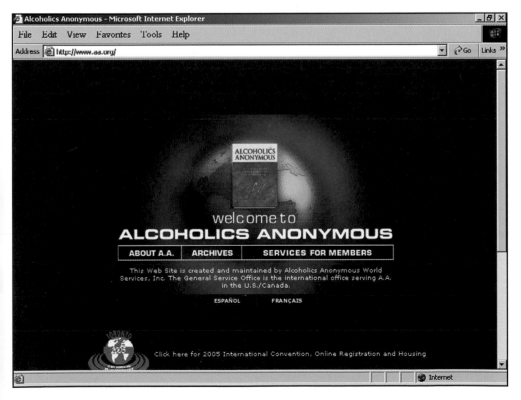

▲ Alcoholics Anonymous is a time-tested organization that helps those who wish to stop drinking reach the goal of staying "clean and sober," one day at a time.

His parents were upset, but Vic refused to worry. He lived for weekend parties and dates with cute girls. If Vic had a problem at school or at the market where he worked, he blamed it on his teachers or his boss. After high school, he enrolled at the local junior college, but school bored him. He dropped out, found a new job, and partied with a new circle of friends. He woke up with a hangover a couple of times a week, and sometimes he wished he could do something better with his life.

Vic hit rock bottom the week he turned twenty-one. Seeing his distress, a friend talked him into seeking help. After talking to Vic a few times, the counselor steered him to Alcoholics Anonymous. Vic agreed to go to the meetings but refused to admit that he was an alcoholic. At last, when he did let down his guard, he came face-to-face with the truth: He was sick and needed help. The only way to cope with his addiction, he learned, is to stay sober—one day at a time. After sitting through dozens of meetings, Vic began to feel that he was winning the battle. AA, he says, saved his life.

## ▶ The Warning Signs

Early on, his AA sponsor gave Vic a useful bit of advice. Today, he passes that message on to friends and associates who say they can use alcohol without abusing it. "Learn from the mistakes of others," Vic tells them. "You can never live long enough to make them all yourself."[1]

The first mistake, Vic would tell you, is to take that first drink. If you never start, alcohol can never claim you for its own. The second mistake, should you find yourself drinking too much, is to sidestep the issue. Alcohol abusers often say, "Hey, I can take my liquor or leave it alone." Still, even experts agree that it is hard to tell when someone has crossed from "using" to "abusing." Here is a scorecard you can use to judge the extent of a drinking problem. It does not matter whether your subject is

**Alcohol Screening** Questions

The questions below refer to your use of alcoholic beverages within the past year. Answer the questions as honestly and accurately as you can. Remember, your responses are completely confidential and anonymous. See the privacy policy for more information. **One drink is defined as 12 ounces of beer, 5 ounces of wine, or one standard cocktail (1.5 ounces of 80-proof liquor).**

1. How often do you have a drink containing alcohol?

   Select One...

2. How many *drinks* containing alcohol do you have on a typical **day** when you are drinking?

   Select One...

3. Thinking about a typical **week**, on how many *days* do you have at least one alcoholic drink? (If you don't drink every week, answer for a typical week in which you do)

   Select One...

4. How often do you have six or more drinks on one occasion?

   Select One...

▲ *The first step in determining whether someone is an alcoholic is to review the individual's drinking habits.*

male or female. To keep things simple, let us think of her as a friend who happens to be a girl.

Does Pat . . .

☐ Binge drink (take five or more drinks in a 24-hour period)?

☐ Lie about how much she has had to drink?

☐ Make up excuses for needing a drink?

☐ Drink when she is alone?

☐ Hang out with friends who drink heavily?

☐ Hide her cache of booze where she thinks no one can find it?

❏ Deny things she has said or done while drunk?

❏ Act forgetful and fail to keep promises?

❏ Try to cut back on her drinking, only to fail time after time?

❏ Choose drinking over the activities she used to enjoy?[2]

How many check marks did Pat earn? It only takes one to suggest that she is in trouble. Will she admit it? As Vic would tell you, Pat will almost surely deny that she needs help.

## ▶ Winning the Battle With Alcohol

If you know someone like Pat, try talking to her (or him) when she is sober. Tell her that you are worried about her drinking and want to help. Look her straight in the eye, and tell her how the drinking is hurting your friendship. Finish by telling Pat that you will stand by her—but that she must get help. Then hook her up with a trusted adult. That could be a teacher, a coach, a counselor, a doctor, a pastor, or a rabbi.[3] If you do not know where to turn, call the National Drug and Alcohol Treatment Hotline. Its number is in the back of this book. A hotline counselor will likely refer you to a self-help group such as Alateen or to a health clinic.

Once Pat starts down the road to clean and sober, she must refocus her life. Her first task will be to enlist her parents or guardians in her fight to regain control. Next, she will have to steer clear of parties where alcohol is available. That can be hard to do, for it may mean breaking up with her drinking buddies. Friends who are still hooked will do their best to tempt her to "kick back and have some fun." To fill the gaps in her social life, Pat can turn to sports, dance, crafts, a church youth group, or community service. If she has been letting her schoolwork slide, she can invest some time and energy in getting her grades up. Last, but not least, she must learn to resist peer pressure.

Family counselor Sharon Scott knows how hard it is for teens to say "no" to friends. Figuring out how to deal with peer pressure, however, is a vital survival skill. What can you do when someone you like wants you to do something dumb or wrong? There are ways to stay out of trouble and keep your friends, Scott says. This is her three-step process:

1. *Check out the scene.* Be alert to clues that tell you trouble is brewing. Are your friends acting sneaky? Are they telling you, 'Don't be chicken!' or 'No one will ever know'?

2. *Make a good decision.* Quickly think through the cost of yielding to temptation. Listen to that clear inner voice that knows right from wrong.

3. *Act to avoid trouble.* There are lots of ways to say "no." Try using a bit of humor, or come up with a better idea for having fun. Flatter your friends by saying, "You are too smart (or too nice) to do that!" Whatever path you take, try to escape the "trouble trap" in thirty seconds or less. Otherwise, you may be talked into letting down your guard.[4]

If you feel yourself giving in to temptation, think about this old Chinese proverb:

When friends offer you a beer or ▶ another type of alcoholic drink, it may be hard to say "no." But consider this: Would a true friend push you to do something that you know is wrong?

*At the first cup man drinks wine;*
*at the second cup wine drinks wine;*
*at the third cup wine drinks man.*[5]

Students Against Destructive Decisions (SADD) takes the message from there. "The image of drinking is parties, good times, and being cool," a SADD radio spot tells listeners. "But, the reality is car crashes, missed classes, broken promises, and gripping addiction. Alcohol use is [a major cause of] youth homicides, suicides, and drownings."[6]

SADD also reminds young people that drinking does not make you smarter, sexier, or healthier. Take a few drinks and you are almost certain to do or say something stupid. Even worse, the chances are good that you will wind up hurting yourself and others.

You can take it from there.

*Those who abuse alcohol do not just hurt ▲ themselves. Often they hurt family and friends as well. In the case of drunk drivers, there is a good chance that they will injure or kill one or more innocent victims.*

**binge drinking**—Binge drinking is defined as having five or more alcoholic drinks in a short period of time.

**blood alcohol content (BAC)**—The amount of alcohol in a person's bloodstream. A BAC of .01 means that there is one part alcohol for every 1,000 parts of a person's blood.

**chugalugging**—Drinking an entire container of a liquid such as beer without stopping to take a breath.

**depressant**—A substance that slows down a person's body functions, thought processes, and coordination.

**distilled**—A liquid that has been purified through evaporation and condensation. Certain types of alcohol are made in this way.

**DUI**—The abbreviation for the crime known as driving under the influence of alcohol. Penalties for this crime vary from state to state.

**DWI**—The abbreviation for the crime known as driving while intoxicated. Police departments sometimes use this term instead of DUI.

**fermented**—Liquids that have been chemically altered by the action of yeast organisms. Certain types of alcohol are made in this way.

**fetal alcohol syndrome (FAS)**—A wide range of birth defects caused by the mother's heavy use of alcohol during her pregnancy.

**firewater**—A name for a strong alcoholic beverage.

**hangover**—The effects that a person feels after coming down from a high that was brought on by heavy use of alcohol.

**jigger**—Between one and two ounces (30–60 milliliters) of whiskey. Often referred to as a "shot."

**lethargy**—A state of prolonged drowsiness or sluggishness.

**malt liquor**—A fermented alcoholic beverage similar to beer that is made with malt.

**Prohibition**—A law that makes it illegal to produce, drink, or carry alcoholic beverages. In the United States, Prohibition lasted from 1919 to 1933.

**temperance**—A movement which fought to outlaw alcohol, or to scale back the use and availability of alcohol.

## Chapter 1. "Why Not Me?"

1. "Never Again . . . ," *Think About Drink,* n.d., <http://www.wrecked.co.uk/ott2.html> (February 13, 2004).

2. "The Effects of Alcohol on Endurance Performance," n.d., <http://athletics.ucsd.edu/strength/Team%20Nutrition/The%20effects%20of%20alcohol%20on%20Endurance%20performance.htm> (November 9, 2004).

3. Laurel Graeber, *Are You Dying for a Drink? Teenagers and Alcohol Abuse* (New York: Julian Messner, 1985), pp. 27–29.

## Chapter 2. A Long and Checkered History

1. Stuart Walton, *Out of It: A Cultural History of Intoxication* (New York: Three Rivers Press, 2002), p. 262.

2. "2000 BC Cuneiform Tablets Have Beer Recipe," *Erowid Alcohol Vault,* November 12, 2001, <http://www.erowid.org/chemicals/alcohol_history1.shtml> (April 30, 2004).

3. "Alcohol in History," *Drinking & You,* n.d., <http://www.drinkingandyou.com/site/us/history.htm> (April 30, 2004).

4. Ibid.

5. "Fun Facts: Puritans to Prohibition," n.d., <http://www2.potsdam.edu/alcohol-info/FunFacts/PuritansToProhibition.html> (April 30, 2004).

6. Don Cahalan, *Understanding America's Drinking Problem: How to Combat the Hazards of Alcohol* (San Francisco: Jossey-Bass Publishers, 1987), p. 24.

7. Ibid., p. 25.

8. Ibid., p. 27.

9. "American Alcohol Consumption," n.d., <http://www.dui.com/oldwhatsnew/Alcohol/colonial.alcohol.html> (November 11, 2004).

10. Statistics from "Facts You Should Know," *Campaign for Alcohol Free Kids,* n.d., <http://www.alcoholfreekids.com/facts_you_should_know.html> (April 2, 2004) and "Sweeping Changes Urged to Curb Youth Drinking," *HealthDay News,* September. 10, 2003, <http://www.ajc.com/health/content/shared-auto/healthnews/kalc/51040.html> (April 2, 2004).

11. "Facts You Should Know."

12. "Sweeping Changes Urged to Curb Youth Drinking."

## Chapter 3. Meet the World's "Dirtiest Drug"

1. Stephen Arterburn, *Growing Up Addicted: Why Our Children Abuse Alcohol and Drugs and What We Can Do About It* (New York: Ballantine Books, 1987), p. 12.

2. Don Cahalan, *Understanding America's Drinking Problem: How to Combat the Hazards of Alcohol* (San Francisco: Jossey-Bass Publishers, 1987), p. 5.

3. Katherine Ketcham and William F. Asbury, *Beyond the Influence: Understanding and Defeating Alcoholism* (New York: Bantam Books, 2000), p. 14.

4. *Safe Driving for Mature Operators: Student Manual* (Heathrow, Fla.: AAA Traffic Safety Dept., 1998), p. 83.

5. Daniel Reyes, "Drowning in Drink," *Sex, Etc.,* April 6, 2004, <http://www.sxetc.org/index.php?topic=Stories&sub_topic=Alcohol+and+Drugs&content_id=1618> (April 21, 2004).

6. Ketcham, p. 15.

7. Ibid., pp. 19–20.

8. Stuart Walton, *Out of It: A Cultural History of Intoxication* (New York: Three Rivers Press, 2002), pp. 292–294.

9. Ketcham, p. 38.

10. Raymond V. Haring, *Myths, Mysteries & Management of Alcohol* (Sacramento, Calif.: HealthSpan Communications, 1995), p. 21.

11. Meridith Salisbury, "A Sober Choice Prevents Fetal Alcohol Syndrome," *Sex, Etc.,* February 2, 2004, <http://www.sxetc.org/index.php?topic=Stories&sub_topic=Alcohol+and+Drugs&content_id=1629> (April 21, 2004).

## Chapter 4. Alcohol in the Marketplace

1. "Youth Bombarded with Radio Alcohol Ads," February 3, 2004, <http://www.jointogether.org/plugin.jtml?siteID=AFK&p=1&Tab=News&Object_ID+568916> (February 4, 2004).

2. "Beer Industry Too Closely Tied to College Athletics," *The Desert Sun,* March 11, 2004, <http://www.thedesertsun.com/news/stories2004/sports/20040311022247.shtml> (April 21, 2004).

3. "Under the Influence," *Common Cause Report,* n.d., <http://www.commoncause.org/publications/booze6.htm> (April 30, 2004).

4. "Youth Risk Behavior Surveillance—United States, 2003," *Morbidity and Mortality Weekly Report,* May 21, 2004, <http://www.cdc.gov/mmwr> (May 30, 2004).

5. "Facts You Should Know," *Campaign for Alcohol Free Kids,* n.d., <http://www.alcoholfreekids.com/facts_you_should_know.html> (April 2, 2004).

6. "Dedication," *Campaign for Alcohol Free Kids,* n.d., <http://www.alcoholfreekids.com/au_dedication.html> (June 2, 2004.)

7. *Alateen,* n.d., <http://www.al-anon.alateen.org/Alateen.html> (February 4, 2004).

## Chapter 5. Learn from the Mistakes of Others

1. "Learn from the Mistakes," n.d., <http://www.quotationreference.com/quotefinder.php> (June 6, 2004).

2. "Kids and Alcohol," *Kids Health,* July 2002, <http://www.kidshealth.org/kid/stay_healthy/body/alcohol.html> (February 4, 2004).

3. Ibid.

4. Sharon Scott, "Reversing Peer Pressure," *Teen Contact,* n.d., <http://www.teencontact.org/peer.htm> (June 3, 2004).

5. Burton Stevenson, ed., *The Home Book of Quotations* (New York: Dodd, Mead & Co., 1967), p. 492.

6. "Media Sample PSAs," *SADD Sample PSAs,* n.d., <http://www.saddonline.com/psa.htm> (November 15, 2004).

Canfield, Jack, Mark Victor Hansen, and Kimberly Kirberger. *Chicken Soup for the Teenage Soul on Tough Stuff.* Deerfield Beach, Fla.: Health Communications, 2001.

Egendorf, Laura K., ed. *Teen Alcoholism.* San Diego, Calif.: Greenhaven Press, 2001.

Haring, Raymond V. *Myths, Mysteries, & Management of Alcohol: Facts, Answers, and Insights About Drinking.* Sacramento, Calif.: HealthSpan Communications, 1995.

Ketcham, Katherine and William F. Asbury. *Beyond the Influence: Understanding and Defeating Alcoholism.* New York: Bantam Books, 2000.

Kinney, Jean. *Loosening the Grip: A Handbook of Alcohol Information.* Boston: McGraw-Hill, 2000.

McGuire, Paula. *Pre-Teen Pressures: Alcohol.* Austin, Tex.: Raintree Steck-Vaughn, 1998.

Richards, Pamela G. *Just the Facts: Alcohol.* Chicago: Heinemann Library, 2001.

Steins, Richard. *Alcohol Abuse: Is This Danger on the Rise?* New York: Twenty-First Century Books, 1995.

Walton, Stuart. *Out of It: A Cultural History of Intoxication.* New York: Three Rivers Press, 2002.

Wijnberg, Ellen. *Alcohol. Teen Hot Line Series.* Austin, Tex.: Raintree Steck-Vaughn, 1994.

## Phone Numbers to Call for Help

*Al-Anon and Alateen Family Groups*
(888) 425-2666

*Mothers Against Drunk Driving (MADD)*
(800) 438-6233

*National Clearinghouse for Alcohol & Drug Information*
(800) 729-6686

*National Council on Alcoholism and Drug Dependence*
(800) NCA-CALL, (800) 622-2255

*National Drug and Alchohol Treatment Hotline*
(800) 662-HELP, (800) 662-4357

*Smart Recovery*
(866) 951-5357

*Students Against Destructive Decisions (SADD)*
(800) 787-5777